Fa
Advertising 2019

————— ❧❧❧❧ —————

*Marketing your social media
to create a live business*

Gary Loomer

Table of Contents

INTRODUCTION 1

CHAPTER 1: WHY IS FACEBOOK ADVERTISING GOOD FOR YOUR BUSINESS.. 5

SO MANY PEOPLE ARE ALREADY USING FACEBOOK 6
TARGET YOUR ADS DIRECTLY TO YOUR CUSTOMERS....................... 6
SET THE GOALS THAT WORK BEST FOR YOU................................... 8
IT IS EASY TO TRACK YOUR FACEBOOK ADS 9
THE BASICS OF FACEBOOK ADS & HOW THEY WORK 11
  How Facebook Ads Work 11
  Who Should Use Facebook Ads? 11
  Low-Friction Conversions.. 12
  How to Target Facebook Ads.. 12
RETURN ON INVESTMENT VS. COST 14
  Why is the Return on Investment so Important? 14

CHAPTER 2: DEFINING YOUR GOALS 17

CAROUSEL AD FORMAT 26
SINGLE IMAGE AD FORMAT 27
THE SLIDESHOW AD FORMAT 27
THE CANVAS AD FORMAT 27
CREATING YOUR FUNNEL 28
  Step 1: Content Creation.. 30
  Step 2: Market to Your Warm List First: 31
  Step 3: "Look-a-like Audiences" 32
  Step 4: Promote to Cold Leads.. 33
  Step 5: Re-Market and Catch Everyone............................ 33
  Who is Your Low Hanging Fruit?....................................... 35
  What is a Good Campaign?..37

CHAPTER 3: FACEBOOK GROUPS EXPLAINED AND WHEN TO ADVERTISE IN THEM 39

OPEN GROUPS.. 39
CLOSED GROUPS 40
SECRET GROUPS.. 40
FACEBOOK PAGES BRIEFLY EXPLAINED AND WHEN TO ADVERTISE IN THEM 42

CHAPTER 4: UNDERSTANDING THE ANALYTICS AND REPORTS 45

A/B TESTING 48
GEO-TARGETING 50
SEASONAL AD CAMPAIGNS FOR AN EXTRA BOOST 51

CHAPTER 5: CREATING YOUR FIRST AD CAMPAIGN 53

FACEBOOK PIXEL EXPLAINED & HOW TO SET IT UP 53
Accessing Your Tracking Pixel Through Your Ads Manager
.. 54
Set up Facebook Pixel 55
Activate the Pixel.. 57
How to Check If the Pixel Program Is Working 58
Facebook Ads Manager 59
Creating Your First Live Ad 62

**CHAPTER 6: FACEBOOK ADS REPORTING AND
OPTIMIZATION 67**

LOOKING AT FACEBOOK ADS REPORTING...................... 67
HOW TO MANAGE THE AD REPORT'S COLUMNS 69
HOW TO DO ADVANCED REPORTING 70

**CHAPTER 7: TIPS TO MAKE YOUR FACEBOOK ADS
CAMPAIGN SUCCESSFUL..73**

MINE THE INSIGHTS YOU GET FROM YOUR AUDIENCE 73
CREATE A UNIQUE AD SET FOR EVERY AUDIENCE 74
ACCOMPANY YOUR ADS WITH A LANDING PAGE 75
USE IMAGERY THAT IS STRIKING 75
SELECT THE RIGHT PLACEMENT TO GET A BIGGER REACH 76
ESTABLISH YOUR BUDGET AND YOUR BID STRATEGY 77

CONCLUSION 79

Introduction

Congratulations on purchasing *Facebook Advertising 2019: Marketing your social media to create a live business.*

The following chapters will discuss:

- **Facebook Advertising 101**
  There are two billion people using Facebook every month which makes it one of the biggest and best platforms in the entire social media network for businesses and enterprises to advertise and promote their products and services to targeted audiences. Facebook Ads can turn out to be very beneficial for your business or enterprise because Facebook has 1.47 billion daily users and 2.23 billion monthly users; this allows businesses to laser target their favorable and profitable audience because everyone is on Facebook nowadays. Businesses can set crystal clear goals for the future while using Facebook Ads. Facebook Ads are a lot easier to keep track of. It makes it easy to trace the success rate of any ad campaign and it also makes it rather simple and easy to figure out the number of "sales and leads"

derived completely from your Facebook ad campaign.

- **Facebook Advertising Strategies For Success**

  How are you going to "Define your goals"? In this section, we'll be shedding some light on advertisement strategies best for you and your audience. Once you understand why is it so essential to advertise on Facebook, The fundamentals of Facebook Ads and how they work, and even your return on your investment. Now you'll want to define your goals and objectives for advertising. Without a solid game plan, you will never achieve anything with your ads.

- **Facebook Pages and Facebook Groups**

  In this section, we have explained the concept and answered some questions about the key aspects of Facebook "Groups" and "Pages".

  - *What Are Facebook Groups? What Is The Best Time to Advertise in Them?*

The most interesting feature of Facebook is that it enables you to make groups and join groups. The social network has groups for everything, For Example, groups for dating, groups for buying and selling, groups for parenting, and countless more.

- ***What Are Facebook Pages? What Is The Best Time To Advertise In Them?***

  Pages that do not symbolize or represent an official cause or person are Known as Community pages, and these pages are keen to cover a long queue of things, from political drama to basic hustle, Usually, the thing or the product of discussion and entertainment embodied by such pages is something that is owned by an enterprise or individual or can't be easily claimed.

- **Optimizing Your Ads**

  How to understand the Analytics and Reports?

  In this section, we are going to explain thoroughly about the process of understanding and utilizing analytics and reports and answer question like

- ***How Often Should You Advertise? What is A/B Split Testing? What is Geo-Targeting?***

  The First thing you'll see when you open the "Facebook Insights analytics" tool is the "Dashboard" also known as the "Overview". When you look at the left sidebar, you'll notice a collection (list) of the many areas of Insights.

- **Creating Your First Ad Campaign**

  This section we are going to learn about Facebook Pixel, For example, What Is Facebook Pixel? How to Set It Up? Why You Need Facebook Pixel? We're going to go over everything you need to know about Facebook Pixel, including what you can do with it, how to install it, and tools that can make the process a little easier.

We hope you enjoy this book!

Chapter 1: Why is Facebook Advertising Good for Your Business

Facebook is the most known and used social media network in the world with 2 billion monthly active users.

Over the last decade, the world of digital marketing has changed remarkably altered. In the past decade, Facebook was originally designed as a way for college students to keep up with each other. But it soon grew to become a worldwide community to share news, pictures and more in one place. It doesn't matter where you are located throughout the world, you can get onto this network and connect with the people who matter most.

Why invest in Facebook Ads and how is it a reliable platform where you should invest your marketing dollars? If you are still unsure as to why you should hop on the Facebook Ads bandwagon, below are four key reasons why Facebook Ads can be a profitable asset for you and your business.

So Many People Are Already Using Facebook

Facebook is a widely used social media website and it has users from all parts of the globe. There are more than 2 billion people who use this social media site each year, and almost 1.5 billion of these users are on each day. This presents a huge market for your business, and Facebook Advertising gives you the tools to reach these customers.

Not only does Facebook provide you with a very large audience to advertise your business to, but this audience is extremely diverse. You can find almost any kind of customer you want on this platform. While 18 to 20 year-olds are the most prevalent users of this platform, the older demographics are growing as well. With the help of Facebook Advertising, you will be able to reach your customers, no matter who they are.

Target Your Ads Directly to Your Customers

Because of the large number of users available on Facebook, you get the benefit of being able to reach your customers, no matter who they are. And Facebook Advertising makes it easy for you to target your ads directly to your chosen customers.

Fortunately, Facebook commercials and advertising provides us with the ability to be able to target the customers to whom our ad will be in front of. Some targeting options you can use are:

- Interests and activities generated from what the user comments on, the apps she/he installed, shares, clicks on, as well as likes.

- Demographics that can be broken down by geographical, location, gender, age, etc.

- Main pages visited and viewed on your website (retargeting).

- Based on the activity on Facebook, you can use "Behaviors" you can also use 3rd organization partner information (data) from Datalogix, Acxiom, and Epsilon. The data involves device usage, purchase activity, and travel preferences.

- Records in your database of the subscribers' and/or purchasers' emails.

Facebook allows you to ask them for finding other related users, known as "Lookalike" audiences, something we will discuss in the following chapters after you have created an audience understanding and using the options I've given you.

Facebook's capability of collecting information based on the interests and concerns of the users, combined with their capability of targeting, makes Facebook an amazing option or method for advertising.

Set the Goals That Work Best for You

When it comes to working with Facebook Ads, there are two types that you can work with. Both of these are designed to help you achieve different goals, so you must make sure that you are fully aware of your goals before you get started.

The first type of Facebook Ad that you can create is an Engagement Ad. An Engagement Ad is when you want to have your customer take a specific action or interact with a post that you put up. This information can then be used to help you learn more about your customers, provide content to your customers, and make sure that you are providing the best customer experience to everyone. This Engagement Ad type is going to rely on the customers actually responding to your content and providing you with information to grow your business.

You can also work with the Direct Respond Ads. These are the best ads to go with when you want to use the campaign to generate more leads and sales for your business. These ads are specifically going to contain some kind of offer, along with a take action cue, in order to get the customer to respond. It could have a link to "sign up" "click here" or "call now". This call of action is important to make sure that your customer knows what you want them to do.

Before launching the ad campaign, first of all, decide what is the purpose of your ad campaign and then "Facebook's goal setting options" can be used to make sure that you complete that task/goal.

It is Easy to Track Your Facebook Ads

It is very important to track the success rate of each and every launched ad campaign. It is very important to estimate the number of sales and leads produced entirely from your Facebook ad campaign.

The process is similar to other ad networks and is simple.

The first step to set up "Facebook conversion tracking" is copying your particular tracking pixel and including that to each and each page of your site.

Once this is done, you'll have to choose from two options for "tracking conversions":

1. Using a web page "URL" you need to track custom conversions. For instance, you

need to track sign-ups to a demo page; you will copy the URL of the page after the sign-up page and set Facebook to track that page (it would be a conversion).

2. Using Event codes for "Event tracking". This option is a little bit technical because what you'll need to do is to copy a little bit of JavaScript (just a line) and stick it at the end of the pixel code "(before the `</script>`)" on the webpage you need to trace. For instance, if you need to trace demo sign-ups, then you need to copy the "Lead Event code", that is "`fbq('track', 'Lead');`" Then you need to stick this code before the `</script>` of the pixel code on the "demo sign up thank you page".

If the steps mentioned above seem advanced and hard to understand, then there's another option, the code and directions can be e-mailed to the developer.

The Basics of Facebook Ads & How They Work

How Facebook Ads Work

There are many varieties of Facebook Ads, nowadays. You can use them to advertise your Pages, content on your Pages, the activity of users, and also your own website. Even though Facebook is growing their focus towards local ads and preserving traffic on its site, you can still be successful in sending users to your website.

Derived from the location, demographics, and profile info of users Facebook Ads are targeted. Only Facebook provides these particular options, no other platform cooperates this much. After your done creating an ad, you need to set a fixed "budget and bid" for every click on the ad or the first thousand impressions that your ad will gain.

Who Should Use Facebook Ads?

Just because some businesses are not a fit for "Facebook advertising" they fail dramatically. You should also keep in mind that you always have to carefully check latest marketing channels, particularly before the demand clouds up the prices, but also make sure that your business model is fit to work with the network.

Ads on Facebook seem more like "display ads" than "search ads". They can be utilized to produce demand, not actually to fulfill it.

Facebook users are on Facebook because they want to connect with their friends, and relatives not for finding products to purchase.

Low-Friction Conversions

To be successful with Facebook Ads your business will want users to "sign up", rather than asking them to purchase your products or services. You need to use a "low-friction conversion" to succeed.

The traffic to your website was never seeking your product. They clicked your ad on a sudden impulse (action). If you depend upon the traffic to purchase something right away or to make your adverts ROI (return on investment) positive, you are going to completely fail.

Facebook users will carry on with their old habits on the platform, irrespective of you trying to convince them to buy your product or service. Rather, simple conversions are a lot easier to stick with for users such as signing up for your provided services, a short form to fill out, or Leaving behind an email address.

How to Target Facebook Ads

Marketers make a lot of mistakes whilst using Facebook Ads, the biggest and the most common mistake they make is not targeting the Ads properly.

On Facebook, targeted users can be listed by their:

- Location

- Gender

- Age

- Connections

- Interests

- Relationship Status

- Education

- Language

- Workplaces

Depending on your targeted audience, each option can be put into use. We recommend that marketers should prioritize concentrating on age, location, interests, and gender.

The "Location" enables you to target users in those countries, states, cities, or zip codes that you provide service to.

The base of "Age and gender" targeting will be on your current customers. For example, if women ranging from 25-44 are the majority of your customers (leads), then start off by only targeting them. If the results prove to be beneficial, Invest in expanding your targeting.

Return on Investment vs. Cost

Why is the Return on Investment so Important?

The return on investment is one of the performance measures that you can use. It can help you balance whether an idea is the best option for you. All endeavors that you take will cost some money to start. Your return on investment helps you to determine if the amount you spent is worth it. If you spend $10,000 on a campaign and you only bring in two customers, for example, then this was probably not a good return on investment.

To move your social media marketing campaign forward there is no single barometer that can guide you better than ROI (return on investment). Because you want to know about your Facebook marketing campaign results, For example, is it generating profit, leads and attracting paying customers? Is it worth the time and effort you put into it?

The formula for the return on investment: "ROI = (Gain from Investment - Cost of Investment) / Cost of Investment"

In this formula, "Gain from Investment" indicates about the gains and profits generated from the sales of the investment of interest. Because "ROI" is measured in percentage, we can easily compare it with returns (profits) from other investments, this allows you to measure various types of investments with other investments.

Chapter 2: Defining Your Goals

Now that you know why you need to advertise on Facebook, The basics of Facebook Ads and how they work, and even your return on your investment. Now you want to define your goals and objectives for advertising. Without a solid game plan, you will not have the success with your ads that you want.

In this Chapter, I will teach you the various types of objectives you can set and achieve with your ads, and which specific types of ads are going to help you reach the goals you set.

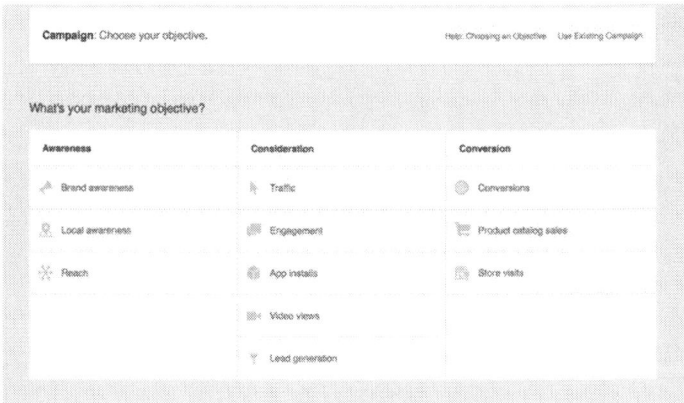

Campaign: Choose your objective.		Help: Choosing an Objective Use Existing Campaign
What's your marketing objective?		
Awareness	**Consideration**	**Conversion**
Brand awareness	Traffic	Conversions
Local awareness	Engagement	Product catalog sales
Reach	App installs	Store visits
	Video views	
	Lead generation	

(image 1)

The beautiful thing about the "Facebook Ads Manager" is that it pretty much lays out the potential objectives for each campaign for you. They even make recommendations on how to go about executing each of them.

As you can see from this screenshot (*image 1*) of the Facebook Manager, there are three main Categories, Awareness, Consideration and Conversion and then there are subcategories under each of the main headings. We are going to examine each of the subheadings in more detail.

Main Category: Awareness
Sub Category: Brand Awareness
Use This When: Your target audience are people who compliment and add value to your own business if you share their content.

You will want to focus on "brand awareness" as an objective if you want to help people find your website or Facebook page. These people generally are not acquainted with who you are and what you do just yet. This is your opportunity to set how often you want people to see your ad and visit your site, which is increasing brand awareness. Typically, you can choose anywhere from 1–90-day intervals for the ad reappearing in your target audiences newsfeed. You don't want them to see it too much or they are likely to tell Facebook to stop showing your ad. I'm sure you have done it a few times yourself?

Main Category: Awareness
Sub Category: Local Awareness
Use This When: You can only service a specific geographic location, you have a physical brick and mortar location, you need to increase sales or are having a grand opening.

This is an extremely useful objective if you are only focusing on certain states and/or cities. Maybe you don't sell online, but you have an actual store. For example, if you are a chiropractor or a restaurant owner. If you just opened, run an ad targeted at residents within a certain mile radius of your restaurant and let them know of your grand opening and specials! If you have multiple locations, you will need to make sure you have an ad for each separate location.

Main Category: Awareness
Sub Category: Reach
Use This When: You need to increase page likes, you want to get more

engagement on your page and posts, or you are starting a new product line with new customers.

The reach is related to the number of people who could potentially see your ad. This is an ad you want to run when you cannot seem to get enough people to like your page, or you find that you just aren't getting the engagement and exposure that you want, in order to build authority and have conversations with your prospects.

Main Category: Consideration
Sub Category: Traffic
Use This When: You started a new vlog/blog, you have a new website design, and you launched a new product line or service.

This is pretty straightforward. Traffic means real people, not bots that you can buy on Fiverr.com from overseas. This is getting actual Facebook users to click on your ad and be taken to whatever landing page, site, or Facebook group/page (Which we will discuss later), you want. Facebook's design allows you to create a call to action button and the most commonly used one for people to be redirected is "Learn More". More traffic to your site ultimately boosts your Google ranking so you show up in search results sooner. Awesome, right?

Facebook Help has very clear instructions on how to set up a "Call-to-Action" Button so I shall not repeat them here.

To add it to your website, contact your web developer or simply choose one from the available options in your website editor.

Main Category: Consideration
Sub Category: Engagement
Use This When: You need to get some feedback on a specific topic, you have something noteworthy you want to gain a lot of views on, and you have a need for dialogue among your page followers.

Page likes are essential. Do you remember when you were a kid, and we would all gravitate to the person who was liked the most? It's kind of the same concept. When you don't have likes or a lot of engagement, nobody wants to be the first one...so it's best if you create this ad to encourage it! You can get ultra-specific in this objective's settings about the type of engagement you want.

Main Category: Consideration

Sub Category: App Installs
Use This When: You need to introduce or get more downloads of a mobile app or a desktop app. You need more interaction with your app for revenue.

If you are a restaurant, or a consultant, or anyone that has a mobile app, this is the ultimate objective for you to monitor and pay attention to developing. This pushes the download of your app to the target audience you set. There are limited options about what it says, the default, is "Install Now", and that will take them to whatever app store your app is on. Be sure you have both an iPhone and Android app on each marketplace or you might lose customers right from the start. If you have a desktop app as well, you can push that in a different ad at a different interval.

Main Category: Consideration
Sub Category: Video Views
Use This When: You don't want to use video views until you have already established yourself as an authority with the brand awareness objective. You need an audience to engage with and take through your sales funnel by adding more value along the way.

If you haven't seen a Russell Brunson ad on Facebook, then you aren't on Facebook. This is the ultimate use of video that today's online marketers are using with the Video View ads. It has been proven, that video posts on Facebook get more engagement, and they are shared at least seven to eight times more than posts that don't have video.

Main Category: Consideration
Sub Category: Lead Generation
Use This When: If you get visitors but they don't take any action; you need to get new subscribers to your list

This is one of the things that most online marketers love most about Facebook Ads—the built-in lead generation functionality. This refers back to the Call to Action button feature you set up earlier. You have the ability to change what that text says. So make it count!

Main Category: Conversion
Sub Category: Conversions
Use This When: You have something to give in order to get an email address from your prospect but they have to go to your website or Facebook page first and they have to click on your call to action

The natural progression of a sale is: you establish yourself as an authority, your audience knows how you can help them, but they just aren't that sure how to justify the expense or just talk themselves out of actually getting the help they need. That's ultimately our jobs, right? To help a customer alleviate some problem? Whether it's time, health, money, hunger. So this ad is geared at taking those already familiar with you and converting them into paying customers and clients. If you are simply sending people to your website, you will want to make sure you have your Facebook Pixel's properly installed, which we talk about in Chapter 5.

Main Category: Conversion
Sub Category: Product Catalog Sales
Use This When: You have physical and tangible products in an online store; Holidays/Sales/Promotions; You want people to see your product features in more detail.

If you look at Microsoft, they have several products and suites, and software packages available. It is useful if you are able to do this as well. This allows you to feature multiple products within the same ad. You can set up a direct link for each product/service and even individual images. You are going to have to set up a catalog in the initial stages of your "Business Manager" Account setup prior to being able to run this ad.

Main Category: Conversion
Sub Category: Store Visits
Use This When: You have a brick and mortar storefront; you have multiple locations and you want to track individual store sales.
This is quite similar to the local awareness objective, but this adds a tracking element to the mix. It's on the phone! Yep! Your customers will access a real-time app with location enabled, and voila! You get real-time data every time someone enters your front doors.

Whew! Lot's of information so far. Let's keep going, we have a lot more to cover. So now that you have your objectives laid out, you need to move on to decide what ad format you will use. This can't be done until you have completed all of your objectives. It's the way the "Business Manager" is set up.

No matter if you sell candles or $5,000 computers, there is an ad format for your particular type of business. Facebook is great for the variety of categories. You might want to stick with one particular ad type without the help of a professional as combinations of the different formats have proven to be quite tricky, especially when just starting out.

There are five types of formats that you can use for your Facebook Ads. These include single video, slideshow, canvas, carousel, or a single image. Here is a breakdown of each of the ad formats. You will need to decide which one is best for you based on the objectives you have:

Carousel Ad Format

If you want to show more in one ad, this is the choice for you. This particular ad format is not only available on Facebook, but you can also use it on Instagram as well. You can feature 10 individual photos and/or videos and each can have a separate, clickable link. The idea is to tell a story with each product and image in the one ad. You can choose the order of each product you list, or you can let Facebook do it, using optimization techniques. Do not opt-in to this feature if you are trying to tell a chronological story with your products, otherwise, it will be random and not make much sense to those who view it.

Single Image Ad Format

This is a standard, one image ad with a standard format. A headline—a place for the description and the ability to add a link to an outside source.

Single Video Ad Format: Expert online marketers will use a single video ad to simply increase their engagement with their followers. Even though YouTube is a video site, Facebook has far outshined them as the leading video sharing platform. Crazy to think right?

The Slideshow Ad Format

Much like the carousel ad format, this type of ad format is just like what it says, it is a slideshow of static (still)images. These are a little quicker to load than video ads, so if you are dealing with a demographic or location that might not have high internet speeds, your best bet it is to choose this format not to discourage your audience.

The Canvas Ad Format

This is an exclusive mobile open type of ad. You can use

If you have ever used Canva before, this is quite similar you can add a variety of different formats like mp3, buttons, and even video. It is faster than even the slideshow to load and is great for building brand awareness. You can see examples on youtube. If you go to youtube and search for "Canvas Ads in Action".

Be sure that you sit down and establish your goals and objectives before you begin any other step in the advertising process. I suggest you start simply with the Awareness category and nothing else and then build on that as you get familiar with the platform and as a way to ultimately guide buyers through your sales funnel based on where they are in their buyer's journey.

Creating Your Funnel

Ultimately, the purpose of advertising on Facebook is to get conversions right? That requires a process or funnel that will help you convert those inquiries into customers. Facebook provides you with an advanced feature that allows you to get ultra-specific about your ad targeting. That makes getting in front of the RIGHT people, at the right time, extremely effortless.

No matter where your customer is in their buying journey, you can rest assured that there is an advanced feature that can help you to put your product and service in front of them at the right time.

According to Statista: "Facebook advertising revenue worldwide from 2009-2017 is $39.94 million U.S. dollars." That number is not going to go down any time soon, which means that as more and people get ahold of this information and take advantage of the advertising benefits, you are going to have to do more to stand out from the crowd. If you start off with a detailed plan and funnel then you will have no problems surviving the advertising world of Facebook.

One of the things marketers feel is the worst thing about Facebook Ads is that the ad performance is highly dependent on creativity and customization. They couldn't just use what they had been using or try to create a cookie-cutter ad with a one size fits all mentality. When in actuality, we come in all shapes, colors, sizes, backgrounds, etc. Literally.

Here are the specific steps you need to take to start creating your Facebook Ads funnel, but before you even consider starting a funnel, I recommend you identify who your target audience actually is. It is not often an overnight process. In the next section, I will cover how to identify your low hanging fruit, but for now, just know that the funnel starts with knowing who is buying your products and services.

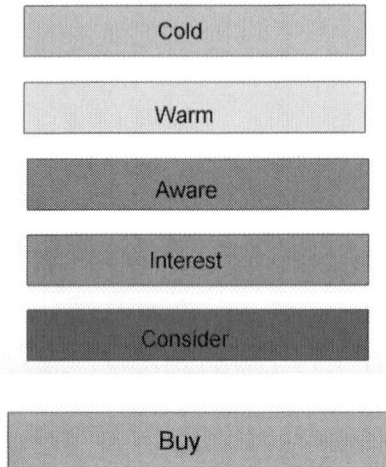

Cold

| Warm |

| Aware |

| Interest |

| Consider |

| Buy |

(image 2)

Step 1: Content Creation

As we mentioned, not every buyer is the same and not every buyer is at the same buying stage in their individual buying journey. You can learn more about the buyer journey from this article: https://blog.hubspot.com/sales/what-is-the-buyers-journey

The content you create in this initial step needs to be segmented. For example, if you are trying to go after chiropractors, lawyers, and dentists, each of those professions has their own set of routines, habits, needs and most importantly language or way of communicating with peers and others.

You aren't restricted to the types of content you share. In fact, it is best if you mix it up between videos, images, articles, blog posts, whitepapers, e-books, etc.

As long as it is most relevant to your audience and you remain consistent, then you are already off to a winning strategy.

Whatever you share on Facebook, be sure you are going to add it to your website as well, you will need to make sure you have it visible for Stage 4 and Stage 5 leads that come through your funnel.

Focus on helping them to solve a common problem or hit a specific pain point, or simply answer a question or break down a complicated topic in your field that nobody wants to touch.

It has to be engaging. You don't want to make the material so boring that people don't want to read it or actually absorb it. Using a variety of ways to deliver the content and keeping it entertaining and informative is a great way to provide valuable content on a consistent basis.

Step 2: Market to Your Warm List First:

Targeting people who have had some exposure to you and your brand is not only an opportunity to get new business, but it's great practice on what to change, what to strengthen and what to add or remove for your next campaign. If the audience that has some familiarity with your brand has a positive reaction to your ad, and you get some great engagement and posts then you know it's going to be ok when you get to Step 5, and targeting the "cold market" as well.

Step 3: "Look-a-like Audiences"

Create a Custom Audience ✕

How do you want to create this audience?

Reach people who have a relationship with your business, whether they are existing customers or people who have interacted with your business on Facebook or other platforms.

Customer File
Use a customer file to match your customers with people on Facebook and create an audience from the matches. The data will be hashed prior to upload.

Website Traffic
Create a list of people who visited your website or took specific actions using Facebook Pixel.

App Activity
Create a list of people who launched your app or game, or took specific actions.

Offline Activity [NEW]
Create a list of people who interacted with your business in-store, by phone, or through other offline channels.

Engagement [UPDATED]
Create a list of people who engaged with your content on Facebook or Instagram.

Store Visits [NEW]
Create a list of people who have previously visited your business locations.

(image 3)

The term "Look-A-Like Audiences" began with Facebook marketing. Facebook has taken a lot of time to build up their artificial intelligence to be able to laser target on the customers you want to find. They are primarily used to reach out to new people who have not been in contact with you or your brand. They simply meet your criteria of low hanging fruit. You can narrow down how similar between 1 and 10 percent.

Step 4: Promote to Cold Leads

The same audience that you used to test out your ad, your "warm" market, you now want to take that content and expose it to your "cold" market. This will enable you to capture new leads and add them into your sales funnel.

Step 5: Re-Market and Catch Everyone

Facebook refers to this concept as "Custom Audiences". It simply means that when a person goes to your page or website and takes some form of action, they get coded, by whatever method you have installed, in order to track their buying behavior online. Here's an example. Have you ever bought something on Amazon and the next thing you know, you see ads for the same thing on the right panel inside of Facebook next to your newsfeed? That is what remarketing is. It is a way of simply reminding people what they are missing out on.

There are 3 types of remarketing that you can choose from:
App Activity, Website Traffic, Customer List and.

- **App Activity**: This handy feature lets you target your ads towards an audience based on how they interact with your app. Let's say they leave off of your site with items still in their cart. You can retarget them with ads that feature a nice discount or % off, and/or a similar product that is cheaper.

- **Website Traffic**: This is really cool. Let's say for example you sell camping gear. After you have placed your Facebook pixels on your website pages, then you can specify the audiences you want to see certain ads. So if someone searches for tents, you can expose them to ads related to the camping gear you sell.

- **Customer List**: This feature gives you the ability to load your own lead lists into the platform. This is similar to the upload contacts feature in LinkedIn. The messages can be customized and personalized and will target individuals who are a great fit for what you have to offer.

As we mentioned, you can't possibly begin to know any of this until you know who these people are, where they are hanging out and how to get in front of them on the largest social media platform in the world.

Who is Your Low Hanging Fruit?

Regardless of whether or not you have a big budget for ads, if you aren't reaching the right people, then it really doesn't matter how much money you set aside for advertising. You won't be successful. Nobody wants to advertise on Facebook without seeing an ROI, and it starts with who and the where. Who is buying your products and services and where do they hang out on Facebook.

If you don't know who your ideal customer or "low-hanging fruit" is, you can't provide content with value. That includes your ads. Not just your posts and blog posts. While demographics like where they live and what gender they are, are nice, they aren't enough in today's competitive marketplace to drill down and be specific to which you can help.

It just is not a strong enough call to action or desire, to guarantee any form of commitment or action on their part. There is no WIIFM moment. (What's in it for me). You need to sit down and figure that out for each of the audiences you serve. Here's what the benefit of doing so will do for your campaigns and how to get started mapping that out:

- Video, Written, Audio or Infographic: When you know exactly who your low hanging fruit is, you know what method of content that they will feel comfortable with. Giving them content they want, in the format they want it, is the number one way to conversion.

- Don't Waste Money: If you aren't targeting the right people, your ads aren't going to be successful, and the cost can add up pretty quickly, without seeing any return on your investment.

- The reason that ad blockers are so popular is that people are tired of seeing things that they don't find important at the time, or aren't relevant to them and their lifestyle. For example, a 70-year-old woman might not want ads for baby food. In a recent survey over 35% of online buyers want to be wowed and have a personal experience with the brands they buy from.

For these reasons, it is critical to evaluate what your target audience wants, as want will beat out need every single time. Look at where they are spending their time. What are they reading, what are they liking, what groups do they belong to, what stage of the buyer journey are they at, who are they following that is a heavy hitter in the game already and what organizations, clubs, and associations do they belong to?

This is going to require you to be a bit creative or you can hire someone to do this research for you. There are plenty of ways to scrape leads from the various social media sights and get insights about their behaviors. Once you know where they are, it's time to get your game face on. Get your content in front of them with Facebook Ads.

Each and every single one of us has a "why" for buying something. And it's not the same for any given two of us. Someone who you have spoken to on the phone and engaged with is not going to take as much convincing as someone who is just finding you through one of your ads for the first time.

Everyone has a specific level of information that they need in order to make an online buying decision. It's the nature of the jungle.

The key to surviving it is superior ads that take your buyer on their own journey allowing them to easily flow down your sales funnel. Do not use copyrighted images and videos, and be sure they are not low resolution. So let's talk about the other things that make up a good campaign.

What is a Good Campaign?

I'm going to use an example and break them down so you know what makes these great and see how the big boys do it. What you see is absolutely everything you can do with your "Business Manager Account" as well.

Paypal:

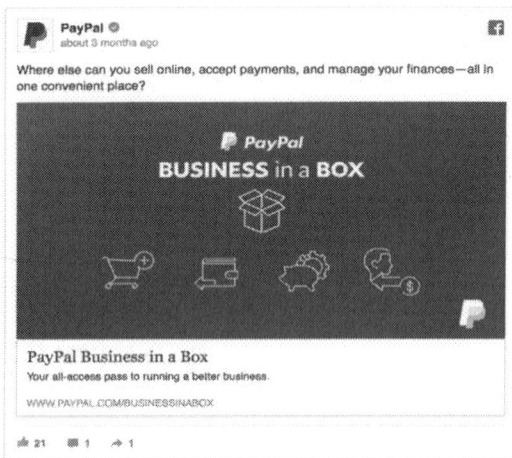

(image 4)

Now while you may think that this looks pretty, well, dull, it does have its distinct advantages. PayPal is sending a simple and appealing visual. This Deep purple is said to be calming in nature and stand for greatness, majesty, affluence, I can go on and on, but I think you get the point. Using the color purple here is a great psychological play on PayPal's part. The color purple has been proven to stimulate creativity, calms your nerves and your brain activity, and evokes feelings of holiness. The Short Title is Under 5 Words or less and the sub-title is as descriptive as a paragraph. Nailed it!

If you're enjoying this book, I would appreciate it if you went to the place of purchase and left a short positive review. Thank you.

Chapter 3: Facebook Groups Explained and When to Advertise in Them

Facebook's ability to create and join groups makes it an even more interesting platform. Countless Groups are on the social network for every purpose you can possibly imagine, For example, groups for dating, groups for buying and selling, groups for parents, and many others.

As we know, there are many Open groups on Facebook, but while open groups exist there are also Closed and Secret groups. In this chapter, we are going to cover all types of Facebook groups and how they are different from each other and we will also show you how to find closed and secret groups.

Now you must be wondering what is meant by "Open, Closed, and Secret" Facebook Groups?

The three types of Facebook groups are: "open, closed, and secret". All of these groups have some aspects and functions in common. The purpose of these groups is to allow users to share memories, organize events, and chat with their friends and relatives, although, some differences are there.

Open Groups

These types of groups as you can guess by the name are accessible to everyone on Facebook. It means that everybody is allowed to see the name of the group, location, members of the group, and posts within the group. The most important point is that everything that is posted (content) in the group is accessible in Facebook searches (navigation) and it is also present in the "news feed".

To join an Open Group, you don't need an invite or approval.

Closed Groups

By comparison, Closed Groups add some restrictions. Similar to Open groups, the name, description, and the member list of a Closed group are available to everyone. Closed groups' can also be found in "Facebook searches".

These groups are called Closed Groups for a reason, new members need to get approved by an admin or receive an invitation from a current member of the group. Moreover, only current members are able to see what the latest fuss is about in group posts and also in its news feed.

Secret Groups

Secret groups go by their name, as they are the completely private out of the three types of "Facebook groups". Nothing related to a secret group is visible to the public, only admins can add new members or they can be invited by current members of the groups to join, and only the members of the group are able to see posts in the group with or without comments. Although, members who have willingly left the group are still able to find the group in the search box and view its name, description, and location.

Visit "Facebook.com/Groups" and rush all over the immediate recommendations. This is Facebook's "Discover" feature for finding Groups for your interest.

At the beginning of the page, there are different niches for groups, such as, "Animals, Science and Tech, Neighborhood and Community, Arts, Travel", etc. Choose any niche to discover Groups both on international and local platforms.

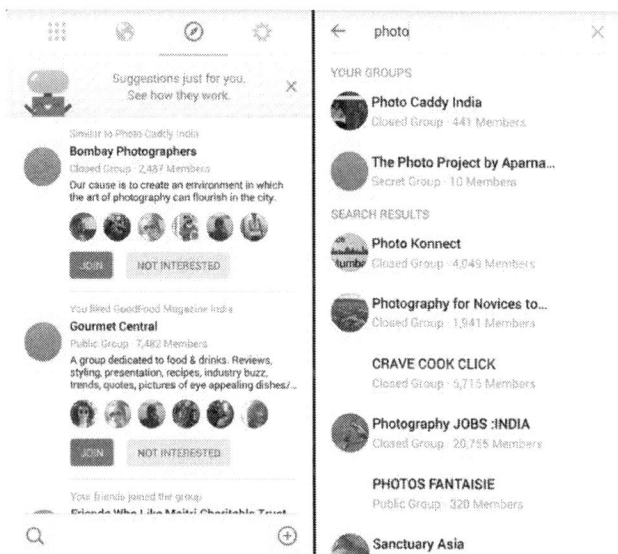

(image 5)

If you really want to go for it, you can start a group of your own, just know that is a long-term strategy. As you interact in other groups you can encourage them also to join yours, never to leave a group.

It is not recommended to advertise in groups directly like in pages. Groups are rather used to build a "community and authority" that benefits you and your business by driving traffic to your personal pages and sites. Believe me, people will observe you for once, and if the entire content on your website, "your landing pages, are ready and dashing, all the links are working and you have a method to pick up calls and catch emails quickly", then you will surely hook them up at least into a chat or dialogue (the inquiry stage).

Facebook Pages Briefly Explained and When to Advertise in Them

A Facebook Page is going to be a profile that you make public. It can be used for a business, a brand, for celebrities, causes, and any other organization. Unlike your own personal profile page, these Facebook Pages are not going to concentrate on gaining "friends." Instead, you concentrate on "fans" or others who will choose to "like" your page.

Your page can have as many fans as you want. Larger companies could have many thousands of fans who want to follow them. This is different than a traditional Facebook personal page that has a cap at 5000 friends. These Pages will work similarly to your personal profile though. You can post updates, place links on the page, have events, and even upload videos and photos.

When you update your Facebook Page, this information will show up right on the page. Fans can choose to come to visit your page and see this information whenever they want. These posts will also show up on the news feeds of your fans if they liked your page.

On your page you're the master at the sail because you have the power to advertise as much and often as you like, you can guide others about advertising their businesses only on specified days of each week to get more and more interaction and page likes.

The most important thing in this chapter you need to keep in mind is that groups never allow you to laser target users (leads) with your ads. However, you can, do this by using a "Page" even if you don't own a website for your business.

Chapter 4: Understanding the Analytics and Reports

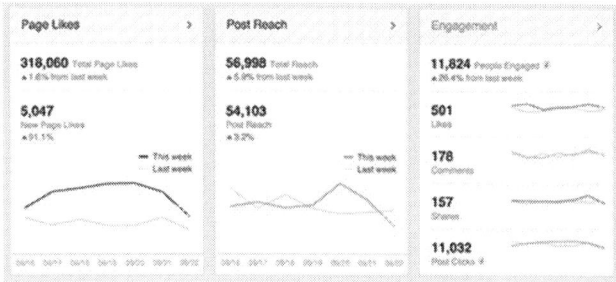

(image 6)

When you first open Facebook Insights, this is what you see—the dashboard (overview). To find the list of areas, look to the left sidebar of the Facebook Insights Features.

Take a quick look at these options:

- **Promotions**

  Giving " boost" to your post is how you can keep an eye on your promoted post and see how well they are performing. Depending on the goal you have, you can create a new promotion and there are a few options you will have.

- **Followers**

  If you need to find how many people are currently or new followers you have or how many have unfollowed you, this is to find that information.

- **Likes**
  To find the total likes you have for your page, paid ads or unpaid ads, who liked or unliked and the location of the like.

- **Reach**
  In this area, you can find how many likes, find who has reacted and the number of comments about your post, how many hides you have or how many Reports, the number of Spam and Likes your post has.

- **Page   Views**
  To find which sections of your page are being viewed the most. A good idea would be to break down by Age, Gender City, and Country or you can use a device.

- **Page Previews**
  Age and gender is a good way to find who has previews your page.

- **Action on Page**
  To find what actions were performed or by who which device was used, the website or link the action came from or direction look under this option.

- **Post**

  To view your own post, not only yours and other pages you follow.

- **Events**

  If you're posting Events to your Business page, you will use this section to find the demographic and how has made a purchase.

- **Videos**

  Facebook Video Analytics, will show you the overall views of each video you posted. You can also find out how long the video was viewed in this section.

- **People**

  Get to know your audience, which demographics they are in or the language, when you look under the Page View and Page Preview tabs.

- **Messages**

  To find the number of conversation and your response time to people on messenger, also the percentage of messages that were blocked, deleted or marked as spam, look under this tab.

Ad frequency is not exact and you will notice that the "average number" is mentioned by Facebook. There's no real guarantee for anyone to reach for your ad to be seen, for example, a user can see your ad once and another may see it three times. Fortunately being exact isn't relevant and way an A/B Split Testing is important when advertising.

A/B Testing

Another type of testing you can work with is known as A/B testing. This is a strategy where you will release two versions of your ads, each having slight differences, to see which one the audience responds to better. The goal of this kind of testing is to make sure you are going with the right type of ad before putting a lot of money into a campaign. This testing could be used for a marketing email, advertising, web pages, and your business.

A good idea before making your holiday ads and launching is testing different content to target your audiences. Facebook Split Testing can be used in the Ads Manager or the Power Editor to accomplish a good ad. Launch sample videos and pictures ads, to control the formatting that will be seen and which ads are more appealing to customers. Test different actions to see which gets the most clicks, importantly you want to find how your loyal customers respond to each ad and which one is more appealing to them and which is more appealing to new customers

(Examples)
An ad can be viewed differently, to two different age groups, but if the ad is formatted correctly

and testing is done correctly then both groups will get the idea of the ad.

Testing an image of a middle-aged woman, instead of a younger woman say in her twenties would not be perceived in the same way. So testing is important and worth trying before advertising. Even though A/B Testing is mainly common sense, it is important for an ad's demographic audience

As you start advertising on Facebook you will run into many things that you will want to test such as images, bidding methods, targeting audiences, campaign, etc. One of the mistakes newcomers make when advertising is wanting to test everything and have too many variables. Ex) This means too many ads and will be too time-consuming and will take weeks to conclude. When this occurs you are left with 2 options; Either create smaller ads with different variations or to use an external ad that is designed for A/B Testing.

After starting a new budget my suggestion would be to use a new managing tool to create new ads this will make your life easier and save you money and time

(Example)
An ad with a middle age couple would probably not work best when I make ads for my hairline better than a younger twenty-something-year-old group of friends out shopping at a hair store, versus a group of middle-aged women having tea and lunch, doesn't have anything to do with the

hair business. So, learn how to keep a watchful eye out for trends and to relate to your audience.

Geo-Targeting

Geo-Targeting is a way to pin a certain audience for a specific geographic. It is one of the most direct ways to get your message across and have a very effective and powerful to boost your efficacy. With just a few clicks on Facebook, you have a new ad that's ready for advertising. But of course, there's a catch there is no easy route when conducting business. Taking this route can really jack up the price of your campaign.

Attracting higher value customers, businesses can benefit from this method whether it's a real estate company looking for a higher source or a B2B business looking to amplify a higher average, to attract new business that will pay more for the growth of the company.

Your business can use this method to help them find some new customers. You can place your physical location and then make advertisements to local customers. With regular outbound sales, this process could cost you thousands of dollars. But Facebook Ads can do the work for you without all the hassle.

In order to target the group that you want, you can just set up an ad with Facebook as usual. When you get to the audience, you can drop a pin in the area where you are located. This shows the program where you are located and that you want to reach other customers in the same area.

After you have dropped the pin, make sure to work with the radius slider. This is going to let you pick how far away you want customers from this area.

So, if you want to reach customers that are within an hour of your location, you can move the slider bar to sixty miles out. This ensures that you get the best possible reach with this feature.

Seasonal Ad Campaigns for an extra boost

Facebook marketers have an array of tools to rely on for help generate leads, there are a few big ones that we need to take a look at.

Targeting Options

Though you can target users using the location, age, Gender or interests to find out people who like your page or app, by searching families or certain people within a household to target a specific ad. You will be able to do this by uploading your own audience, to similar people of your already targeted audiences.

Facebook's Cross-Border Insights Finder to compare data between the use of International Customers to compare data and unlock opportunities.

You can target specific shoppers for the holidays between Thanksgiving and New Year's Day. Facebook identifies holiday shoppers, by the specific post about Black Friday and Cyber Monday and keep in mind that you aren't just targeting shoppers who are only buying gifts but those who are also looking for something for themselves. Self-gifting is becoming quite popular according to a Facebook survey, of course, if you're having trouble finding an audience start with your target.

Another suggestion Facebook recommendation is to go through your customer database to better understand your audience and demographics of past holiday history to reach those buyers again or new buyers.

Use the Facebook Audience Insights tool, to better understand customers and purchase behavior if you haven't already launched a new ad. Using this information you can effectively target users and creating ads that will be more appealing to customers and potential customers.

Facebook users are now making more purchases using their mobiles. 61% of shoppers between Black Friday and Cyber Monday are found to be males using Facebook. Facebook holiday shoppers are known to use their mobile more during the holiday, to receive free gifts with their purchase.

People are known to use their smartphones in stores to compare prices, compare products, take photos re-review and get discounts. Consumers will have plenty of choices when making their holiday purchases.

Chapter 5: Creating Your First Ad Campaign

Now it is time to go through and create your very first ad campaign. This process is pretty simple to do. And once you complete the process one time, you will be able to go through it over and over again and it will only take a few minutes to complete. Make sure that you have information about your target audience, a good idea of your budget, and more in place ahead of time to make sure you can speed up the process.

Facebook Pixel Explained & How to Set It Up

There are two distinct Facebook pixels; the conversation pixel, and the tracking audience. Facebook combined these 2 one upgrade tracking pixel. In this section, everything you need to know about Facebook pixel will be discussed, including how to install it, how you can do it, and tools that can make the process easier.Why would you need Facebook pixels? Facebook's tracking pixel has two major capabilities to track users who took action because of your Facebook ad and to track activity on your site. If you're running Facebook Ads, you should install the pixel.

Let's look at the first purpose: alone this is worthy of installing pixel because of measuring the licks to your site, (you'll actually be able to see your users' actions, that maybe signing up or making a purchase.) You'll actually be paying for the conversion. If you aren't getting the results you want, troubleshoot your ads more effectively: you know that the ad is great but something isn't quite cutting it for your customers. Due to specific action on your site (like visiting certain pages or not complete their purchase), it can help you target messages to warm audiences., making your ad more relevant, lowering your relevance score and saving you money.

To find your tracking pixel ads each Facebook account gets one-pixel which you'll install on every page, but different from the old tracking pixel where you would have to install the different types of tracking pixels for each image (conversation, one for views, etc.) on each page.

Accessing Your Tracking Pixel Through Your Ads Manager

When "creating pixel" just names the order to create the new pixel. You will see a note after signing up for a business manager and have the options.

Set up Facebook Pixel

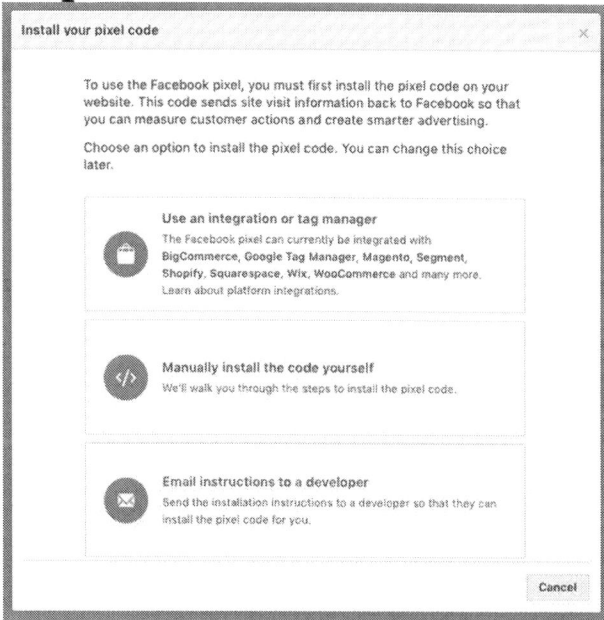

(image 7)

From here, you can make a few choices for how to install and use your Facebook Pixel tool. The options you can choose from include:

- Get some instructions emailed to you from the developer

- Install the code manually. You will need to know some coding to do this method.

- Use what is known as a tag or integration manager.

At this point, you need to click on the button for "Use an integration or tag manager. This allows you to see if Facebook was able to match up with your website platform. If you see that your site builder is listed there, you are in luck. The rest of the setup for Pixel is going to be really simple.

Look for your platform and then follow the instructions that come up on the screen.

There are times when your website builder won't be listed on the menu. You may also not have a developer who can send you the instructions. When this happens, you will need to go through and manually install the pixel. The steps that you need to do this include:

Click on "Manually install the code yourself".

Look through the new menu. It is going to show you the next three steps you can follow. The steps are going to vary based on the computer system you use.

You will be able to see the code you need for Facebook Pixel as the second step. This is the base code and you need to install it on each page of your website to make it work properly. The platform that you use for your business website is going to determine how many more steps you will need to use.

Many people use WordPress to create their business websites. This platform is nice to work with because its free plugin, known as PixelYourSite, will make it easy to install this program on each page of the website, and you only need to push one button.

NOTE: If you are using another platform besides WordPress, you will need to find the instructions for that site. This is going on the presumption your website is in WordPress.

Go to the plugins menu and search for PixelYourSite.
Click install.

Activate the Pixel

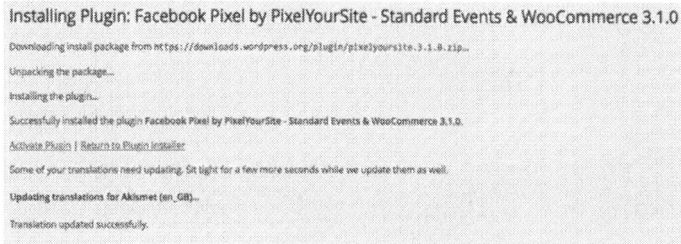

Installing Plugin: Facebook Pixel by PixelYourSite - Standard Events & WooCommerce 3.1.0

Downloading install package from https://downloads.wordpress.org/plugin/pixelyoursite.3.1.0.zip...

Unpacking the package...

Installing the plugin...

Successfully installed the plugin Facebook Pixel by PixelYourSite - Standard Events & WooCommerce 3.1.0.

Activate Plugin | Return to Plugin Installer

Some of your translations need updating. Sit tight for a few more seconds while we update them as well.

Updating translations for Akismet (en_GB)...

Translation updated successfully.

(image 8)

After this plugin has been installed and you have time to activate it, you should go to the dashboard for PixelYourSite. Here you need to take the Pixel ID and enter it into the right section. If you are not sure what your Pixel ID is, you should go back to the manager for your Facebook Ads. There is a Pixels tab there on the top corner under the name of your Pixel. Copy that number and then paste it into the dashboard.

After the Pixel ID is in place, scroll to the bottom of the screen so that you can Save Settings.

After you finish these steps, you will have Facebook pixel installed on your site. The next time someone comes to your website, whether they get there from email, search, or social media, they will be tagged by that pixel and matched up on Facebook. This helps you to build up the custom audience based on the people who have visited that site.

How to Check If the Pixel Program Is Working

The next thing to do is make sure that the Pixel program is working. To do this, you need to head back to your website and let a page load up. From here, you can go back to your Pixels tab, which is back in the Ads manager. There should be a green dot there that will say when your pixel was last active. It should have the time when you last loaded a page of your website.

Now that you took the time to create one of these Pixels and it is installed on your site, you can now take that information and build up a custom audience. This custom audience is going to include demographics of those who have actually visited your website.

To create this custom audience, you can go back to the Ads Manager and click on "Pixels" again. In the dashboard, you can click on "Create Custom Audience. You will see a pop up that appears that says something similar to "Create custom website audience."

For now, we are going to work on a custom audience, but will try to keep it simple. We are just going to create an audience out of everyone who has visited your site. Make sure that you select the Pixel and that you see a green dot there. This means that it is active. You can also keep the "all website visitors" part clicked. Take a look at how many days are in the field. You can pick between 30 to 180 days depending on your needs. A good rule of thumb here is that when you are doing a retargeting campaign, the more days from when someone last came to your site, the lower CTR you will have. Make sure to give this audience a name so you can remember it.

After this information is set up, you can click on create an audience. There will be a new message that comes up that alerts you that this audience is created. You can always check on that new audience with your Audience tab, located right next to the Pixel tab we used earlier.

Facebook Ads Manager

The next thing that we are going to look at is Facebook Ads Manager. This is free for you to use. Facebook asks that you set up a campaign with the help of Ads Manager though (we do not suggest that you use Power Editor because it is the more complex tool. You would not want to use this method because it is used by agencies and enterprise- level advertisers.) When using the Facebook Ads Manager you can:

Ad sets and new ads can be created Facebook ad bids can be managed

Different audiences can be targeted

Ad campaigns can be optimized

Campaign performances keep track

Facebook ad campaigns can be a/b

Facebook Ads Manager accounts have 3 ways to be Access: bookmark the link for quick access, click on the drop-down arrow that can be found in the upper right corner and "Manage Ads" located in the drop- down menu however

However, Facebook suggests playing around with the Ads Manager to see what you would find.

When you get to this step, you will want to click on the Facebook Business Manager. From here, you can gain access to a lot of useful information. You can see information about all your reports, your audience on Facebook, and more. You will want to check out this part of your Facebook Ads account.

Some people make the misconception that budget is all that matters. Now you're asking for trouble to approach you and very quickly I might add! Instead, you should check that the results you get is worth what you are spending on that campaign (ex) $69 per bundle -$35 but It's up to you to decide if that's worth it or not for your business or just wasting as space. A number of results you are getting are also an important factor. If you are going to put a lot of money and your time into an ad campaign, and you don't get a lot of results out of that campaign, if you're putting time and energy into them and running campaigns, while only getting little results, you may want to consider opting to a different platform or trying new strategies.

People should see your ad a few times before they decide to purchase with you, but if you get 0 to 3 likes, it is safe to say that no one is shopping with you. And over time your relevance score will be affected, you will want to keep a close eye on how active your campaigns and if the frequency keeps getting too high.

You do need to monitor this information, but you don't have to stress out about it as much as the other two options. There is some really important information that comes into play here that can really benefit you. For example, it is going to help you break down information about your target audience into fields like:

- Location
- Age
- Gender
- Other pages they like
- The interests that they show on Facebook
- Household information, if Facebook has it.

Knowing information about your target audience is very important, and seeing whether the target audience is changing or not can make a big difference in your future marketing endeavors. But it is not really going to show you how effective the advertising is doing. Check on it occasionally, but focus on the other metrics more.

You can view your target audiences, using this data. You might end up getting fresh concepts for new campaigns to run. I personally make campaigns that are aimed directly at customers who I know likes a specific topic and get surprisingly strong feedback.

Because Facebook users spend a considerable amount of time on the social network as a way to be entertained and spend time, unlike Google, where they go for a specific reason (to search for something), Facebook is a far more social environment. And with that social aspect, comes an opportunity for brands to grab the attention of their target audience.

Of course, simply advertising on Facebook isn't enough. You need to know how to create, launch, and analyze that ad so that you can optimize your campaign and increase your ROI for future campaigns.

Creating Your First Live Ad
"How can you start creating a new Facebook campaign?"

To answer this question, let's start with the basics.

You'll be given prompt directions the entire campaign creation funnel (image below). Just put in a few ad details like images and copy for a new ad to be created.

Step 1: Select Your Campaign Objective

In this step, you can choose from some of the options below to help you pick out the right campaign objective.

- Local awareness or reaching customers near you.

- How far you want the reach to go

- Brand awareness

- Lead generation

- Traffic

- Video views and if the video is going viral

- Conversions

- How many customers visit your store

- All installs.

Step 2: Name Your Campaign

Naming your campaign is the next step. This is important because it can help you to keep things organized. No one else is going to see the name of this campaign, so you can pick any name that you want. But pick something that will be easy for you to remember and keep track of. The name tells it all, so you want to be as creative as possible. When you pick out a name for your ad, make sure that you add the date in there somehow. This can be helpful in the future when you want to look back at it and you are trying to find it among a list of other campaigns.

Step 3: Finding the Target Audience

The next step is to pick out your target audience. You can choose to make a new custom audience or you can work with one of your current saved audience. Make sure you take some time to pick out a good target audience. You can easily have a fantastic campaign, but if you are not targeting it to the right people, you won't get any results.

Step 4: How to Set Up Ad Placement

There are several different places where you are able to put your Facebook Ads. The right location can make all the difference in whether your potential customers will actually see the ads or not. Some of the options you have for ad placement include:

- Audience network
- News Feeds
- Instant articles
- In-stream video
- Instagram

When you are setting up a campaign, you can choose to either let the Facebook program do the placement, through Automatic Placement, or you can go through and configure the campaign manually. Facebook often does a good job with ad placements. If you have data that shows another placement would provide you with a better return on investment than what Facebook is proposing, then it may be best to do this part manually. For your first campaign, consider using Automatic Placements to make things easier. The information you glean from this first campaign can be used to help you with making manual campaigns later on.

Step 5: How to Pick Your Budget for Your Campaign

Now it is time to set up the budget for your campaign and begin bidding. Picking the right budget for your project is going to be very important when it comes to how successful the campaign will be. You don't want to put a budget that is too small, or you won't reach the customers that you want. But if you place a budget that is too large, you could waste a lot of money.

When you work with Facebook, you can pick from two main budgeting options. The first option is a daily budget. This is the amount that you authorize Facebook to spend when they deliver your ads each day of the campaign. When you set this daily budget, you are telling Facebook to get you as many results as they can for the budget you pick.

There are times when Facebook will spend more than what you set for the daily budget. But it will even out to give you the average that you set. For example, if Facebook sees that there is a day or two with high-potential for your campaign; it could decide to spend more than you set for the daily budget. This won't go more than 25 percent above that daily budget. Then on days that Facebook sees as low potential, the program will spend less than your budget.

As you look through your daily budget, it is likely that your daily ad spend is going to look more like a lot of curves rather than a straight line. This is normal for your campaign and it just means that Facebook is going through and optimizing the delivery of your ads to the right market.

You can also choose to work with a lifetime budget. When you do this, you tell Facebook the full amount that you want to spend over the lifetime of your campaign. Then Facebook will divide up the total budget of your campaign, keeping it pretty even across all your campaign dates. You will need to tell Facebook the dates that you want the campaign to go so that the program can average out how much to spend every day.

If you're enjoying this book, I would appreciate it if you went to the place of purchase and left a short positive review. Thank you.

Chapter 6: Facebook Ads Reporting and Optimization

After you took the time to set up your very first ad campaign with the help of Facebook, you can pat yourself on the back. But this doesn't mean that the work is done. While Facebook is set up to do a great job with optimizing your campaigns on its own, you will still need to be on top of things and routinely review if everything is running smoothly. Even if the program does a great job on its own, you will learn what works for your ads and can apply these insights into future campaigns. No matter how amazing the campaign is, you must monitor to make sure that it is performing well.

Looking at Facebook Ads Reporting

The easiest method that you can use to help review your campaign performance is to work with your Facebook Ads Manager. In this program, you will be able to filter your campaigns looking at objectives and dates. You can also zoom in on any campaign to measure the performance of every single ad that you have set up.

When you go through this process, make sure that you have set up the right date range when looking at the ad reports. If you are in the wrong date range, you will look at the wrong information and may be confused about what is working and what isn't. You can also take the time to compare two different ranges of dates. This will help you to compare how your campaign performance is doing over time.

The best way to check how your campaign is doing right now is to look over the past seven days. Make sure to click on this when you look at Facebook Ads Manager. If you go for longer periods of time, it may change all your metrics and can make it hard to understand your recent campaign performance. It won't show how things have changed over time; it will just average everything out. If you want to see these changes, then you will need to compare a few dates together.

As you take a look at your Campaigns tab, you may notice that there are reports for different types of metrics. Some of the options that you can choose include the following:

- Unique link clicks
- Impressions
- Cost per conversion
- Cost per click

This is where you are able to check on the complete overview of all your campaigns on Facebook and how they are performing. You can then select a campaign to look at simply by clicking on the checkbox that is right in front of the campaign name. From here, you can navigate to the Ad Sets and then the Ads tabs. This allows you to see the performance of every campaign unit that you have. The neat thing here is that Facebook is set up to automatically display the data that is the most useful for each campaign.

How to Manage the Ad Report's Columns

While Facebook can do a good job of showing you the most relevant metrics for your advertisement, it is possible for you to go through and change some of the metrics that you see in your ad reports. To do this, you simply need to go to your Columns menu and then select the different reports so you can change your metrics.

From here, you can either select the pre-set reports or you can create some new custom reports. To create a custom report, you just need to click on "Customize Columns" and then click on the reports that you want to create.

One of the best things about Facebook is that you can choose from a wide variety of metrics to add to your report. Some of the most insightful reports that could provide you with the most information on your campaign include:

- Performance

- Clicks

- Engagement

- Messaging
- Media
- Website conversions
- On-Facebook
- Apps
- Offline

After you have had time to create the ad reports that are needed to help you fully understand how the campaign is doing, make sure that you save these reports. This will ensure that you can come back to them later and use them for comparison at a later date. You can also make it so these new reports are your default options.

How to Do Advanced Reporting

In addition to some of the metrics that are shown in the Ads Manager reports we talked about above, you can also take your reports and break them down into even smaller details. These details can make the difference in how you advertise and so much more. The Breakdown menu is going to be your best friend to get this done. Some of the ways that you can break down the reports you have for your campaign include:

- **Delivery**: This could include the time of day, the device, the platform, the browsing platform that was used, the location, gender, and the age.

- **Action**: This could include information such as carousel card, video sound, video view type, destination, and conversion device.

- **Time**: You can pick out the amount of time you want to break down out of the report. This can be as long as a month or more, and even down to a day.

With the help of campaign breakdown, your business is going to be able to find out the answers to a bunch of questions that can be useful on this campaign as well as on many other campaigns that you come across. Some of the answers that you will get include:

Which of your ad placement choices are performing the best?

What times of the day, or which days of the week, end up giving you the most conversions at the lowest cost?

What are the best-performing target countries?

To break down the ad campaigns by these different criteria, you will need to go into your Ads Manager account and select at least one of your campaigns. It is possible to click on more than one if you wish. You can then go to the Breakdown menu and select the criterion that you want from the list. For example, you could choose to break down the campaign by Placements, which is going to help you to figure out which placements are not doing the best so you can turn them off and not waste time or money.

Take some time to look around the reporting options with your Facebook Ads. There is so much information available here that it can sometimes seem overwhelming at first. After some time, you will have a better understanding of some of the most important ad metrics and which optimization practices are the best for your campaigns.

Chapter 7: Tips to Make Your Facebook Ads Campaign Successful

When you first get started with Facebook Ads, you may be overwhelmed by all the options that are out there for you to explore. Understanding some of the best tips and strategies that are available with Facebook Ads can make all the difference in how successful your campaign is going to be. Let's look at some of these tips so you can get the customers and the sales that you need.

Mine the Insights You Get from Your Audience

One of the best tools that you can use when creating your campaign is Facebook's Audience Insights. This tool is going to help you learn about your audience ahead of time. This can be helpful if you are just getting started on your business. You don't want to spend a lot of money on targeting an audience that you don't know all that much about.

The Facebook Audience Insight tool can help you to mine the data that is available through Facebook. Since there are so many people on the Facebook network, there is a wealth of information on almost any demographic that you can choose. With this information, you will be able to learn exactly who the target market is and what they like or dislike, based on those who are already fans of your business page.

This can be a great tool for a lot of businesses. Instead of just making guesses and hoping that you are right, you can use this Facebook tool to help you know exactly which users are the most likely to follow through on any call-to-action that you place on your ads. It can save a ton of money and time, making it easier for you to focus on the quality of your ad while avoiding wasting any time with your targeting.

Create a Unique Ad Set for Every Audience

One of the features that you can use on Facebook Ads is that you can choose to create different sets of ads for unique audiences. This means that you could effectively create two different campaigns and then deliver them to two different audiences. Or you can create the same ad and then send it out to two types of audiences that are completely different. This basically ensures that you can get better targeting.

Let's look at an example of this. If you are a retailer who sells kitchen supplies, you may have a nice stainless steel bowl that you want to market to two different target audiences. Instead of trying to send out the same ad campaign to each group, you could create two unique ads and then choose where they are delivered. You may have the first ad go to professional chefs and the second one would be towards mothers who stay at home.

Accompany Your Ads with a Landing Page

There are very few instances where you should connect an ad to your product page or your website without first pushing your visitors over to a landing page. These landing pages can be helpful because they will allow you to maximize the efforts that you put into Facebook advertising by educating your users before you decide to get them to purchase from you.

These landing pages can make a lot of sense because advertising on Facebook isn't always cheap. You will need to spend money on all the clicks and to make it cost effective, you want to make sure each of these clicks counts. Simply sending the customer over to a basic product page or website, without providing them with some clear directions on how they should act from here, could be a waste of your money.

Use Imagery That Is Striking

You are going to find entire courses out there on how you can effectively write Facebook ad copy. While the ad copy is really important, you also need to take the time to pay attention to the images that you use in your ads. Visual content is way more influential than your textual content, so you need to pay special attention to that.

The image that you use doesn't necessarily have to be a picture of your service, product, or business. It could be something that is going to catch the attention of your customer and will get them to read the ad. It is best if the picture is relevant to the product, but it doesn't have to match up exactly. Remember that Facebook doesn't want you to have an image that is over 20 percent words, so make sure that your image is there to grab the attention of the customer, not display your message.

Select the Right Placement to Get a Bigger Reach

When you are working on a campaign on Facebook, you can choose from a variety of platforms, devices, and placements. This gives you a lot of choices and a lot of control over your campaign, and the best choice is going to depend on your goals and the type of campaign that you want to create.

One thing that you can try out is to add Instagram to the video view placement, the engagement, and the reach. This can improve your results by as much as 40 percent. However, when you do this, it is likely that you are going to see fewer comments and likes if you are running it as a Facebook page post ad.

You can also use Messenger here. It is a great add-on to traffic and the conversion campaign. Currently, the Messenger ads are going to perform really well.

Audience Network placements are a great way to increase the traffic and reach for your ads in most cases. But you should pay some particular attention to the key metrics that you have. In some cases, you may want to run a campaign on one device because it can lower the amount that you pay. In some niches, Android users may have given you a higher conversion rate while lowering your cost. This is why it is a good idea for you to run a mobile device test in your niche to see whether that would lead to an improvement in your campaign results.

Establish Your Budget and Your Bid Strategy

And finally, you need to make sure that from the beginning you set up a budget and a bid strategy for your campaign. Otherwise, you will keep the campaign going way too long and you will end up spending more than you intended. Facebook has made this part easy though with the use of Optimized CPM.

With this kind of tool, you are giving Facebook the permission it needs to bid for ad space based on any goals or constraints that you provide to it. This is often the best way for you, especially as a beginner, to maximize your budget and avoid any overspending. Until you are able to get an idea of how much the ad space costs, and how to best allocate your budget, just stick with the Optimized CPM to get the most out of your campaign.

Being able to create a great campaign with Facebook Ads can seem a little bit overwhelming in the beginning, but there are so many great things that you can do when you utilize all the features that come with it. While you do need to think about the ad itself, you must make sure you understand the platform that you are using. Once you determine who you're trying to target, and you have a good idea of how much you want to spend on the campaign, then it is easier to focus on some of the smaller details.

Conclusion

Thank for making it through to the end of *Book Title*, let's hope it was informative and able to provide you with all of the tools you need to achieve your goals whatever they may be.

Going into the book, we have discussed the number of people using Facebook today, and that Facebook is one of the largest and effective platforms in the social media era for businesses and enterprises. We have discussed the difference between the dashboard options, also known as Overview and the 13 different parts of the <u>Facebook</u> Insights analytics tool.

- Promotion
- Followers
- Likes
- Reach
- Page Views
- Page Previews
- Action on Page
- Post
- Events.

- Videos

- People

- Messages

- A/B Split Testing

All of these topics are important to help you create and run your own Facebook Ads campaign. Make sure to refer back to this book to help you get started with Facebook Ads and bring in customers from today!

Printed in Germany
by Amazon Distribution
GmbH, Leipzig